GROSS
BODY
SCIENCE

CRUST

& SPRAY

GROSS STUFF IN YOUR
EYES, EARS, NOSE, AND THROAT

Written by C. S. Larsen

Illustrated by Michael Slack

M Millbrook Press • Minneapolis

To Nancy, Zach, and Alex, the keepers of my heart. To my editor, Sara, for making things perfect. And to all those curious about crust and spray! —C. S. Larsen

To Clarence Locke
—Michael Slack

Text copyright © 2010 by C. S. Larsen
Illustrations copyright © 2010 by Michael Slack

Millbrook Press
A division of Lerner Publishing Group, Inc.
241 First Avenue North
Minneapolis, MN 55401 U.S.A.

Website address: www.lernerbooks.com

Library of Congress Cataloging-in-Publication Data

Larsen, C. S. (Christopher Sterling), 1966–
   Crust & spray : gross stuff in your eyes, ears, nose, and throat / by C. S. Larsen ; illustrated by Michael Slack.
      p.   cm. — (Gross body science)
   Includes bibliographical references and index.
   ISBN 978-0-8225-8964-8 (lib. bdg. : alk. paper)
   1. Mucus—Juvenile literature. 2. Exudates and transudates—Juvenile literature. 3. Earwax—Juvenile literature. I. Slack, Michael H., 1969– II. Title.
QP215.L37 2010
612.8—dc22   2008033777

Manufactured in the United States of America
1 2 3 4 5 6 — BP — 15 14 13 12 11 10

CONTENTS

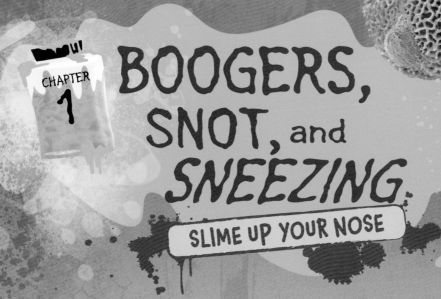

CHAPTER 1

BOOGERS, SNOT, and SNEEZING

SLIME UP YOUR NOSE

Don't look now, but there's a booger in your nose! Don't worry—everyone has boogers (and snot too). Boogers are made of mucus. That's that gunky stuff inside your nose and sinuses. Mucus comes from mucous membranes in your nose. It's normal for mucous membranes to make mucus. It's also very important. Mucus is a great protector against getting sick. All that sticky stuff is a way for your body to catch the germs in your nose. Your mucus also catches other things like dust, dirt, pollen, and small rocks. (OK, it doesn't catch small rocks—unless you've been hiding them up your nose!) Mucus keeps the stuff from getting into your lungs.

Pollen grains get caught in sticky mucus.

GROSS FACT

Did you know that your nose and sinuses make about a quart (1 liter) of mucus every day? Most of it flows down into your throat. *YUCK!* The only other option is for it to go out your nose. *AAACHOO!* Now there's mucus everywhere!

#1

Tiny hairs in your nose also help capture dust and dirt by moving it to the front of your nose or to the back of your throat. Then the stuff can be removed by either blowing it out or swallowing it. Which do you prefer?

A rhinovirus like this can make your mucus multiply.

A BOOGER IS BORN

So what happens when mucus dries up?
It gets all hard and crusty. You guessed it.
That's when a booger is born. **CONGRATULATIONS!**
You're the proud owner of a big, brown
booger. But what do you do with it?
How do you get it out? No, picking
your nose is not a good idea. Never
stick anything smaller than an
elbow in your nose. Besides, there
are lots of germs in there. You
don't want them on your fingers.
The best thing to do is to get a
tissue and blow the boogers out.
Boogers are a good thing. They're
a sign that your nose is working
fine. But that doesn't mean

Blow your nose—don't pick it!

you can flick them at the girl sitting in front of you. **REMEMBER:** She has boogers too. And they may be worse than yours.

THE SCOOP ON SNEEZING

Oh no! Your science teacher just *sneezed* all over your homework assignment. **YUCK!** Is he sick—of grading students' papers all day? Or maybe he's just allergic to the incredible student you are.

Aaaachooo!

Sneezing happens when air is forced out of your nose (and mouth, if it's open) due to a sudden, uncontrollable contraction, or tightening, of your chest, stomach, and diaphragm. But why do you sneeze? Usually it's because of some irritation in your nose.

Computer-generated artwork of allergens— the stuff that makes allergic people sneeze.

Irritation in your nose can make you sneeze.

The mucous membranes in your nose send a signal to the sneezing center in your brain. Then your brain sends a message to all the muscles needed to make the sneeze happen.

A TICKLISH NOSE IS NO LAUGHING MATTER

Just about anything in your nose can cause a sneeze. Dust, cold air, pepper, or a feather can set off sneezing. Some people sneeze at bright lights. Check it out for yourself.

STERNU-WHAT?!?

ACHOO! Sorry for the sternutation! Sternutation is a fancy word for sneezing. But a sneeze by any other name is still a sneeze, right? Globs of snot can fly out of your nose to the other side of the room. So the next time you feel a sneeze coming on, try warning your friends by yelling,

"I'M GOING TO STERNUTATE!"

Did you know that when you sneeze, the air (and snot) in your nose can come out at 100 miles (160 kilometers) per hour? That's about fifteen times faster than you can run. So don't even try to race a sneeze. The sneeze will win every time!

The next time you walk into a bright room or step outside on a sunny day, see if you sneeze. If you do, you're a photic sneezer. That's a name for people who sneeze when they see light.

When should you try not to sneeze? That's an easy one. **NEVER!** Sneezing is a normal body mechanism, just like coughing, blinking, or flying. (Just kidding about the flying. But you really should let that sneeze fly! If you try to stop a sneeze, you may burst an eardrum or give yourself a bloody nose.)

Don't stifle a sneeze—you may wind up with a bloody nose.

GROSS RECIPE: FAKE SNOT

Just what you need—more snot. Have an adult help you with this recipe, as it contains borax. (Borax is a strong chemical. You should never put it near your nose, eyes, or mouth.)

1 Mix $\frac{1}{8}$ cup of borax with 2 cups of warm water. Let the mixture cool for 5 minutes.

2 In a different bowl, mix 2 spoonfuls of school glue with 3 spoonfuls of water.

3 Add 2 drops of green food coloring to the glue-and-water mixture.

4 Pour the glue-and-water mixture into a plastic bag. Then add 1 spoonful of the borax-and-water solution.

5 Squish together until mixed.
YOUR FAKE SNOT IS READY!

Now you can bring the snot to school and fake a sneeze with your friends. Or better yet: Fake one in front of your teacher, and maybe you'll get out of class! You'll most likely end up in the principal's office, though.

GROSS FACT #3

Did you know that there's a world record for the most sneezes in a row? According to Guinness World Records, a young girl from Great Britain once sneezed for 977 days. She sneezed more than one million times!

Sneezes spew out snot, germs, and all kinds of gross stuff!

Even though you shouldn't stop a sneeze, it is a good idea to keep your sneezes from flying across the room and spreading germs all over. The best way to do this is to cover your mouth and nose with the inside of your elbow. Or was it the outside of your elbow? **OUCH!** Definitely not the outside.

COUGH, HACK, and WHEEZE

GUNK IN YOUR THROAT

Cough! Hack! Wheeze! **Are you sick,** or did you swallow a bug? Either way, there's something in your throat or lungs that your body doesn't like.

Coughing is a way for your body to remove unwanted things like dust, dirt, germs, and boring subjects in classrooms. (OK, coughing won't get rid of boring subjects—but it may land you in the nurse's office. Unless you're faking your cough. Then you may wind up in detention!)

Mites that live in house dust can make you cough.

When you cough, you breathe in quickly and then close your glottis— the spot near the back of your throat and at

13

Extreme close-up of the glottis

the top of your trachea, or windpipe. When your glottis closes, air pressure builds up in your lungs. Then you quickly open your glottis and force an explosive amount of air through your trachea and out of your mouth. Kind of cool, huh? So the next time you cough, just blame it on Glottis and Trachea (whoever they are).

I'M GLOTTIS! NOT GLADYS!

TRACHEA HERE.

COUGHING 'TIL YOU PUKE

Coughs come in two types. One type is a dry cough—a cough that doesn't force anything out. This is an easy way to cough, but it's not very productive. After all, the whole idea of coughing is to get something out of your throat or lungs, right?

The other type of cough is called a productive cough. Productive coughs push out whatever is irritating you. If you have a productive cough, you may cough very hard. Sometimes you might cough so hard that you set

HACKING HYGIENICALLY

If a cold or flu has you coughing like crazy, make sure you don't cough on anyone. And don't cough on your hands either. That's just like sprinkling germs on them. Then later, when you shake someone's hand, you end up giving the germs to them as well. COUGHING INTO A TISSUE IS A MUCH BETTER IDEA. Coughing into your elbow works too.

off a gag reflex. When that happens, the food in your stomach can get forced out. Then...well, you puke. Now that's one gag that is no laughing matter!

GROSS FACT #4
Did you know that your cough can travel at 60 miles (96 kilometers) per hour? That's as fast as a car. No wonder germs spread so quickly!

GUNKY, GREEN PHLEGM

If you have a productive cough, you might cough up phlegm. **Phlegm is not the name of a rock band** or a slang word for your little sister. It's a thick, sticky material that's released by glands in your bronchi—the

If you swallow phlegm, it ends up in your stomach!

airways of your lungs. Phlegm can also come from the mucous membranes in your nose and sinuses.

But why do you have phlegm? The sticky mucus is there for a reason, and it's perfectly normal. Phlegm helps remove bacteria, germs, and other nasty stuff from your system. When you swallow the phlegm, all the germs it contains go into your stomach where they're killed by stomach acid. And if you sneeze, the phlegm takes the germs out that way.

Allergens like these can throw phlegm production into overdrive.

But sometimes, when you're sick, your body makes too much phlegm. If you have a runny nose, for example, extra snot might run down into your throat—and that makes more phlegm. **YUCK!** Your body also makes more phlegm in response to lung infections and allergic reactions. When the body makes extra phlegm, it's a sign that something's wrong.

GROSS FACT #5

Did you know that phlegm comes in all sorts of colors? Clear or white phlegm is normal. **Yellow phlegm** may mean you're getting sick. **Green phlegm** usually means you have some type of infection. **Red** or **brown phlegm** could mean that you are very sick. If your phlegm is red or brown, you should see a doctor.

GROSS RECIPE: FAKE SNOT

See the recipe for fake snot **ON PAGE 11.** Fake phlegm is the same thing—it just calls for yellow food coloring instead of green. You can also try other colors for added grossness!

SPITTING UP SPUTUM

When you cough up phlegm, it's called **sputum.** Coughing is normal when you have too much phlegm. It's your body's way of trying to get the slime out. So the next time you see someone coughing in class, **be on the lookout for flying sputum.**

Phlegm becomes sputum when it flies out of **YOUR MOUTH**.

Or if you have phlegm that's coming out of your own mouth, you might try warning everyone by yelling,

"SPUTUM ALERT! SPUTUM ALERT!"

Mucous membranes in the sinuses are phlegm-making machines!

HUMORISM

DO YOU NEED A GOOD LAUGH? Try learning about humorism. OK, humorism doesn't have anything to do with being funny. Humorism is actually an ancient theory about how the human body works. Humorists believed that the body was made up of four basic substances. The substances were black bile, yellow bile, phlegm, and blood. These were known as the four humors. Humorists thought a healthy human body contained equal amounts of all four humors. People believed to have unbalanced humors were sometimes "treated" with **prescriptions of cold baths,** alcohol, or even poisons. Now that's no laughing matter!

CHAPTER 3

EYE SECRETIONS, PINKEYE, and STIES

CRUD IN YOUR EYES

Crusties. Sleepies. Eye gunk. Crud. You've heard all the terms, but what *is* that stuff that sometimes gathers in your eyes?

The hard, crusty gunk that collects in people's eyes is a form of eye secretions. (Secretions are materials that our bodies release—things like sweat and pus.) Most of the time, the tears your body makes wash away your eye secretions. But not always—and especially not at night while you're sleeping. Why?

Tears ooze onto eyeballs to help keep them clean.

These lacrimal glands are where your tears are made.

GROSS FACT #6

TEST Ⓐ

DID YOU KNOW that in one year, you make about 8 pints (3.8 liters) of tears? That's a lot of crying! Thankfully, not all the tears are from sadness. **Tears of joy are included—like the ones you get when you ace a science test!**

During the day, your eyelids blink away eye secretions. Eyelids act like windshield wipers, spreading cleansing tears over your eyes and sending them down into your tear ducts. But at night, your eyes are closed. Then your tears are not being blinked away. They build up. Oils and sweat from other glands

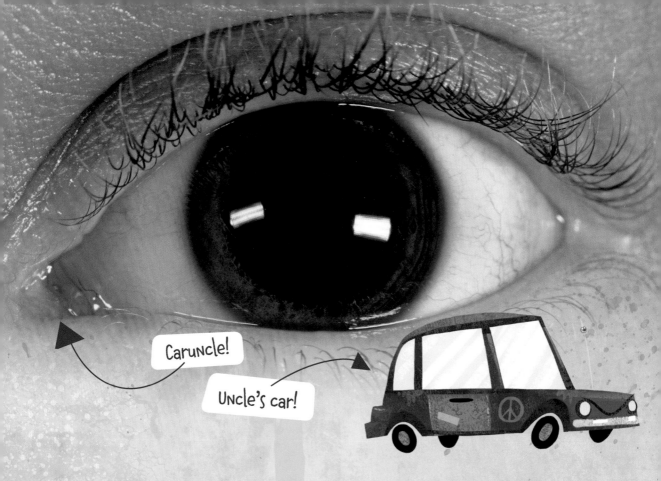

Caruncle!

Uncle's car!

build up too. When enough stuff builds up, it begins to collect in your eyes. Then it can turn into a dry, gunky crud.

Eye secretions usually accumulate near your caruncle. That's that red, fleshy bump of skin in the inner corner of your eyes. It has nothing to do with a car and an uncle—or your uncle's car. **Your uncle and his car are much bigger than caruncles and should never be put in your eyes.**

Caruncles contain oil and sweat glands. **They work a little bit like nets,** catching tears and other substances that build up in your eyes. That's why you might find gunk in them when you wake up in the morning. So there you have it. That's the scoop on eye secretions. They're just a normal way for your body to make sure you can see things clearly. But if you ever do find tons of thick, gooey stuff coming from your eyes, go see a doctor—before you can't see anything at all!

GROSS FACT #7

Did you know that the average person blinks about ten times each minute? That's about a year's worth of blinking during your entire lifetime! Try not to blink too much. Otherwise, you may miss another year!

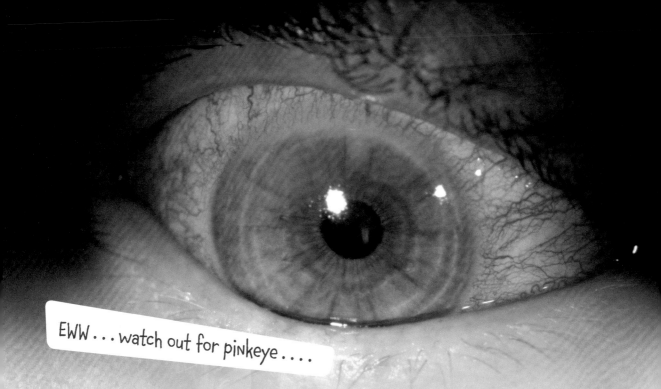

EWW . . . watch out for pinkeye. . . .

WATCHING OUT FOR PINKEYE

You may have heard of someone getting pinkeye. Is pinkeye like getting a black eye? Nope. They're two entirely different things. But neither one is any fun.

Pinkeye is an inflammation in the white part of your eye and the undersides of your eyelids. The inflammation irritates your eye, and it turns a red or pinkish color. The technical term for pinkeye is **conjunctivitis**. It's quite common and usually lasts for about seven to ten days.

What causes pinkeye? The redness can be due to an infection caused by bacteria or a virus. Pinkeye

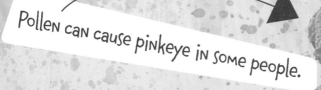
Pollen can cause pinkeye in some people.

can also be caused by
allergies, whether you're
allergic to pollen, dust in
the air, or tough math
homework. (OK, you won't
get pinkeye from doing
homework. But your eyes
may look a little red if
you stay up all night
studying.) Another
reason you may get
pinkeye is because
something's irritating
your eye. That something
could be smoke; dust; or
chemicals, like those found in certain
kinds of soaps.

Some types of pinkeye are contagious. That means
you can catch them if you're around someone who has
them. Other types of pinkeye are not contagious. These
are the types of pinkeye caused by allergies or irritants.

If you do get pinkeye from someone else, be careful
not to spread the germs around to others. Wash your

hands, don't cough on anyone, and try to refrain from wiping your hands all over your science teacher's desk. Don't go swimming in a public pool if you have pinkeye. The infection can spread in the water. **You can't see the tiny germs floating around, but they're there.** Don't share washcloths, pillowcases, tissues, or toothbrushes with other people either. (Come to think of it, sharing these items is a pretty bad idea whether you have pinkeye or not!)

The next time you see someone with red eyes, don't be too alarmed. Pinkeye is common. Just tell the person to get their conjunctivitis eyes down to the nurse's office and **not to touch any doorknobs on the way.** Oh, and say no if the person asks to borrow your toothbrush.

STIES ON THE EYES

HOW GROSS! There's a zit on your eye! OK, it's not exactly a zit that's growing on your eyelid. It's a sty. Sties are another common eye condition. They're bacterial infections that are similar to zits, but they show up near the root of an eyelash. Sties are filled with yellow, sticky pus. Like zits, they can eventually burst. Ouch!

Sty on an eye

So what should you do if you have a sty? Should you squeeze it, sending pus flying across the room? **NO!** It is not a good idea to pop a sty. The pus inside is filled with infectious bacteria. You don't want to be spreading that stuff around. Besides, the last thing you want is to end up with a nickname like **STY SQUEEZER** or **PUS PINCHER**.

Instead, try applying a warm washcloth to the sty. That can help relieve the pain and reduce the swelling. It's also a good idea to check in with a doctor. The doctor may prescribe antibiotic cream to help your eye heal.

CHALAZIA

Sometimes chalazia may show up on your eyelids. Chalazia are lumps that might look a lot like sties. But they are not infections. Instead, they are painless bumps of tissue. Chalazia develop when debris blocks the oil glands in your skin. Chalazia might look gross, but they are not contagious.

What's the best way to prevent sties? **Wash your hands more frequently.** The infectious bacteria can be spread from one person to the next just by shaking hands. Or by touching an infected object, like a book that was used by a person who had sties. Perhaps this very book you are reading now is one of them! *EEEEWW!* See why hand washing is a good idea?

EARWAX, EAR GERMS, and INFECTIONS

CHAPTER 4

GOO IN YOUR EARS

Have you ever thought about that waxy stuff inside your ear? That's earwax, and everybody has it. Some people have a lot. That can make it hard to hear. Others have hard earwax. This can be very painful. But where does earwax come from? And what exactly is it, anyway? Let's take an expedition into earwax to find out.

Earwax is a yellow, sticky liquid. It's made in your cerumen glands inside the skin of your ear canal.

Earwax isn't really wax at all— at least, it's not like the candle wax on birthday cakes. (Now there's a gross idea . . . **earwax candles!**) But earwax is a waxlike substance. And it's very important to your health.

How does earwax help you? For one thing, it keeps dust and bugs out of your ears. It keeps bacteria out too. Earwax works like sticky fly-catching tape. It protects your inner ear canal and eardrum by catching all the stuff you don't want in there. But too much earwax can cause problems. It can interfere with your hearing. Sometimes so much earwax builds up that it completely clogs your ear. Then you can't hear at all.

Sticky earwax on light brown cotton swab fibers

33

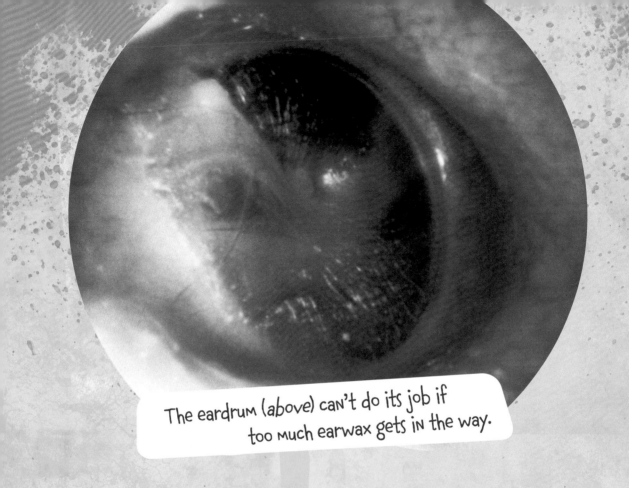

The eardrum (*above*) can't do its job if too much earwax gets in the way.

How does extra earwax affect hearing? It prevents sound from getting to your tympanic membrane, or eardrum. Trying to hear with an ear full of earwax is a little like listening to someone talk through a brick wall. It's just not very effective.

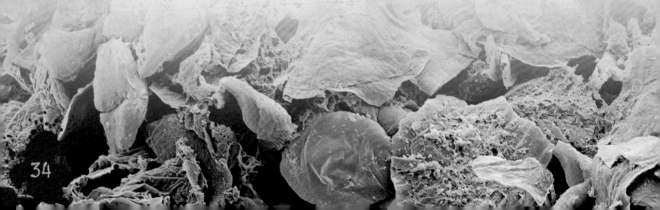

Did you know that about 10 percent of children and 5 percent of adults have an earwax blockage at any given time? HELLO? Can you hear me?? HELLO!?! Perhaps you are one of those 10 percent.

THE PAIN OF CRUSTY WAX

Aside from temporary hearing loss, earwax can cause other problems. The wax can build up into a hard, crusty material. This creates pressure on the inside of your ear. Ouch! Earwax can also cause a tickle in your throat. Your ears, nose, and throat are all connected. This means that whatever affects one can affect the others.

Even though earwax can cause problems, it's a natural, healthful substance. So remember: It's really a *GOOD* thing! And if your earwax does build up, it's an

Magnified earwax and debris inside an ear canal

easy thing to treat. Just make an appointment with your doctor. (But don't try bringing her a cake with earwax candles. It's probably not her birthday anyway.)

HEARING ABOUT EAR INFECTIONS

You have an ear infection. What? You can't hear me? That's because **YOU HAVE AN EAR INFECTION!**

Ear infections can make it tough to hear. And even worse, they can be very painful. Unfortunately, they're also quite common— especially in young children.

Ear infections are caused by germs that get inside your ears. The nasty germs can infect the outer, middle, or inner part of your ear. When that happens, a blockage can develop in your ear. The blockage

OUTER MIDDLE INNER

keeps sound waves from vibrating your eardrum. When sound waves can't vibrate your eardrum, you can't hear very well.

If you have an outer ear infection, you'll have redness and pain in the outside area of the ear (the part you can see). This type of infection is sometimes called swimmer's ear. Swimmer's ear usually happens when you're exposed to lots of water. The water can cause the skin inside the outer ear to get soggy. Then bacteria can build up. Or fungi can grow. (Fungi have nothing to do with being a fun guy. They're living things that often grow in damp environments.)

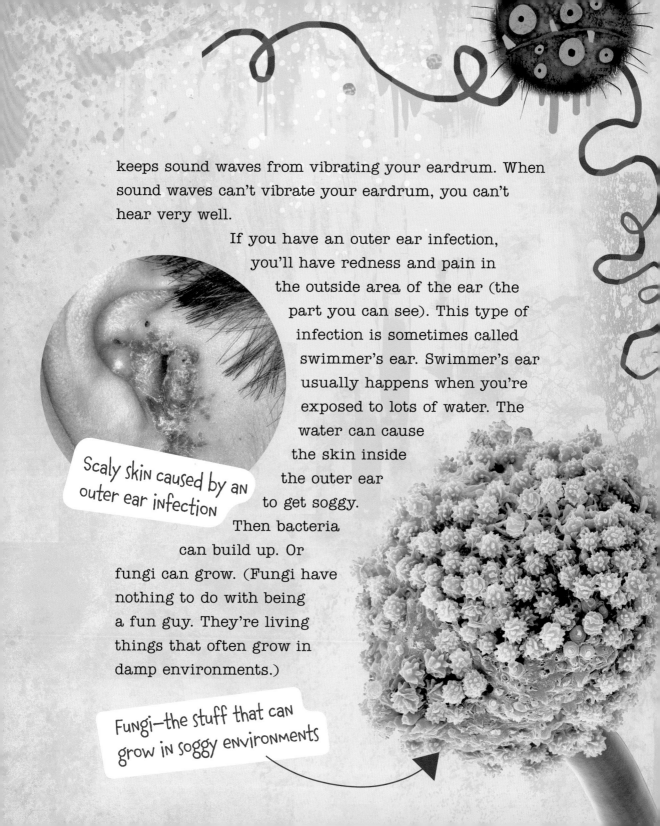

Scaly skin caused by an outer ear infection

Fungi—the stuff that can grow in soggy environments

THERE'S A HAMMER IN YOUR EAR!

Did you know that there's a **hammer** and an **anvil** in your ear? (This may make you wonder if there's also a blacksmith.) The hammer and anvil are tiny bones. They help convert sound into something your brain can recognize. If you have an ear infection, thick, sticky fluid can build up in your middle ear, preventing your hammer and anvil from vibrating properly. Then you may not hear anything but a ringing sound. (Or perhaps that's just the blacksmith in your ear playing the bells!)

Another part that can get infected is the middle ear. Otitis media is the fancy name for middle ear infections. These types of infections can inflame the eustachian tube (another fancy word!).

Close view of an ear infection

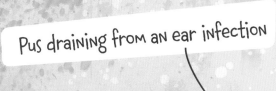
Pus draining from an ear infection

The eustachian tube connects your middle ear and your throat.

If you have an infection in your eustachian tube, fluid or pus can build up. That makes your ear hurt a lot. You may also have trouble hearing. You might end up at the doctor's office if your eustachian tube is infected.

Inner ear infections are known as labyrinthitis. This may sound like a disease you'd catch if you got stuck inside a labyrinth. But labyrinthitis is actually caused when viruses or bacteria make their way into your inner ear. Labyrinthitis can cause vertigo, or extreme dizziness. The vertigo can get so bad that you end up puking—which might help you by leaving a trail out of the labyrinth!

These proteins are on the outside of a rhinovirus. Rhinoviruses cause about half of all colds.

OPERATION HAPPY EAR: PREVENTING EAR INFECTIONS

What's the best way to prevent an ear infection? Don't catch a cold from someone else! Ear infections often come from congestion in your ears and nose—and colds cause lots of congestion. This means you'll want to wash your hands often and avoid picking at your ears or nose.

If you do end up with an ear infection, your doctor can treat it. First, he'll look in your ears with an otoscope. This tool allows the doctor to see your eardrum. When the doctor looks at your eardrum,

GROSS FACT #9

Did you know that 75 percent of children will have had at least one ear infection by the time they reach the age of three? Ouch! Thankfully, ear infections are not as common for adults (although sometimes parents don't seem to hear well—especially when you're asking to play more video games).

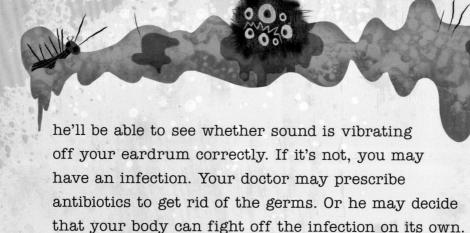

he'll be able to see whether sound is vibrating off your eardrum correctly. If it's not, you may have an infection. Your doctor may prescribe antibiotics to get rid of the germs. Or he may decide that your body can fight off the infection on its own.

Now you know all about ear infections. So the next time your parents ask you to take out the garbage, just shrug your shoulders and explain you can't hear due to otitis media in your eustachian tube. If nothing else, they might be impressed with your amazing vocabulary and take out the garbage themselves. (Yeah, right.)

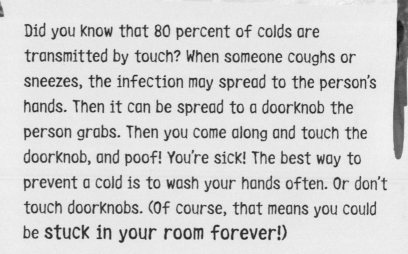

GROSS FACT #10

Did you know that 80 percent of colds are transmitted by touch? When someone coughs or sneezes, the infection may spread to the person's hands. Then it can be spread to a doorknob the person grabs. Then you come along and touch the doorknob, and poof! You're sick! The best way to prevent a cold is to wash your hands often. Or don't touch doorknobs. (Of course, that means you could be **stuck in your room forever!**)

GLOSSARY

antibiotic: a drug that kills bacteria and helps to cure infections

bacteria: microscopic living things that can cause diseases

caruncle: the fleshy bump of skin in the corner of your eyes

chalazia: bumps of tissue that develop when debris blocks the oil glands in your skin

earwax: a yellow, sticky liquid made in glands inside the ear canal

eustachian tube: a tube that connects the middle ear and throat

fungi: living things that often grow in damp environments

glottis: the spot near the back of your throat and at the top of your windpipe

labyrinthitis: an infection of the inner ear

mucus: a slimy liquid found inside the nose and sinuses. Mucus comes from mucous membranes.

otitis media: an infection of the middle ear

phlegm: a thick, sticky material released by glands in the airways of your lungs. Phlegm can also come from mucous membranes.

pinkeye: an inflammation in the white part of your eye and the undersides of your eyelids. The technical term for pinkeye is conjunctivitis.

secretions: materials that our bodies release. Sweat, pus, and tears are secretions.

sinuses: hollow spaces above the eyes and on either side of the nose

sputum: phlegm that has been coughed up

sternutation: sneezing

sty: a bacterial infection near the root of the eyelash

swimmer's ear: an infection of the outer ear. Swimmer's ear usually occurs when you're exposed to lots of water.

trachea: windpipe

tympanic membrane: eardrum. The tympanic membrane vibrates when sound waves strike it, allowing you to hear.

SELECTED BIBLIOGRAPHY

Discovery Communications. *Discovery Channel*. 2008. http://dsc.discovery.com (June 19, 2008).

Mayo Foundation for Medical Education and Research. *Mayo Clinic*. 2008. http://www.mayoclinic.com (June 19, 2008).

MedicineNet. *MedicineNet*. 2008. http://www .medicinenet.com/script/main/hp.asp (June 19, 2008).

Nemours Foundation. *KidsHealth*. 2008. http:// kidshealth.org (June 19, 2008).

Settel, Joanne, and Nancy Baggett. *Why Does My Nose Run?: And Other Questions Kids Ask about Their Bodies*. New York: Atheneum, 1985.

Seuling, Barbara. *You Can't Sneeze with Your Eyes Open & Other Freaky Facts about the Human Body*. New York: Dutton, 1986.

WebMD. *WebMD*. 2008. http://www.webmd.com (June 19, 2008).

FURTHER READING

Branzei, Sylvia. *Grossology and You.* New York: Price Stern Sloan, 2002. Read all about blood, pus, guts, warts, and other gross subjects.

Grossology
http://www.grossology.org
Visit this website for an entertaining look at all things gross.

KidsHealth
http://kidshealth.org/kid
This site is loaded with lots of facts about the human body. It also includes great health information for kids.

Masoff, Joy. *Oh, Yuck!: The Encyclopedia of Everything Nasty.* New York: Workman, 2000. Check out this title for a fun (and gross!) look at topics such as dandruff, body lint, creepy critters, and more.

Solheim, James. *It's Disgusting and We Ate It!: True Food Facts from Around the World and Throughout History.* New York: Aladdin Paperbacks, 1998. Solheim provides a funny overview of some disgusting and unusual meals.

Stangl, Jean. *What Makes You Cough, Sneeze, Burp, Hiccup, Blink, Yawn, Sweat, and Shiver?* New York: Franklin Watts, 2000. Explore the human body, and learn more about why it acts the way it does.

Szpirglas, Jeff. *Gross Universe: Your Guide to All Disgusting Things Under the Sun.* Toronto: Maple Tree Press, 2004. Szpirglas takes a stomach-churning look at mucus, blood, vomit, and lots of other disgusting topics.

Your Gross & Cool Body
http://yucky.discovery.com/body
This site includes information on snot, boogers, earwax, eye gunk, and more.

INDEX

About the Author

C. S. Larsen is an award-winning author of short stories and novels, including the Magic Krystal and Marvin Archibald Trekker series. He lives in Rochester, Minnesota, with his wife, Nancy, and two boys, Zach and Alex.

About the Illustrator

Michael Slack's illustrations have appeared in books, magazines, advertisements, and on TV. His paintings and drawings have been exhibited in the United States and Europe. Michael lives in the San Francisco Bay area.

Photo Acknowledgments

The images in this book are used with the permission of: © Dennis Kunkel/Visuals Unlimited, Inc., pp. 1, 3 (background), 5, 27, 37 (bottom right); © MicroScan/Phototake, p. 4; © Tom Le Goff/Digital Vision/Getty Images, p. 6; © David Mack/Photo Researchers, Inc., pp. 6–7 (bottom); © iStockphoto.com/Sharon Dominick, p. 8 (top); © Lauren Shear/Photo Researchers, Inc., p. 9; © Christina Kennedy/ Alamy, p. 10; © Todd Strand/Independent Picture Service, p. 11; © istockphoto.com /franck camhi, p. 12; © Eye of Science/Photo Researchers, Inc., pp. 13, 14, 20 (bottom); © BSIP/Photo Researchers, Inc., p. 17; © Steve Gschmeissner/Photo Researchers, Inc., pp. 18, 33 (bottom), 34–35 (bottom); © Dr. P. Marazzi/Photo Researchers, Inc., pp. 20 (top), 30 (bottom), 39; istockphoto/Achim Prill, p. 21 (background); L. Bassett/Visuals Unlimited, Inc., p. 22; Scientifica/Visuals Unlimited, Inc., p. 23; © Frank Awbrey/Visuals Unlimited, Inc., p. 24; © Barbara Galati/Phototake—All rights reserved, p. 26; © Pulse Picture Library/CMP Images/Phototake—All rights reserved, pp. 30 (top), 37 (top left); © Qrt/Alamy, p. 32 (top); © Custom Medical Stock Photo—All rights reserved, p. 34 (top); © Brian Evans/Photo Researchers, Inc., p. 38; © Laguna Design/Photo Researchers, Inc., p. 40.

Front cover: (eyeball) © Dwight Eschliman/Stone/Getty Images; (background) Dr. Richard Kessel & Dr. Gene Shih/Visuals Unlimited, Inc.; (woman sneezing) © iStockphoto.com/Sharon Dominick.